MW00931212

How to Pray and Never Run Out of Words

Praying the Scriptures Back to God

A Bible Study In

Six Life Changing Lessons

Dedication

I dedicate this book to the women who have been Godly role models to me and taught me how to pray.

Gail Combs is an international prophet, teacher, and dear friend who has nurtured me through years of heartaches and triumphs. She has been a constant encourager and has opened many doors of ministry for me.

Jane Hanson is President of Aglow International, an organization dedicated to seeing God's kingdom come into all of the earth. She helped me to see God's plans for the nations of the world.

Bobbye Byerly, an international intercessor who taught me leadership skills and challenged me to press in to know God in deeper ways.

Brenda Tullos, is a godly, anointed teacher, and friend. She opened up the word of God for me and taught me to see the Lord high and lifted up and shining in His glory.

Introduction

This Bible study may be used for individual study or by groups. My deepest desire is that those who read this study and participate by filling in the homework for each lesson will come into a deeper relationship with the Lord. I pray the time you spend in this study will grow your relationship with God.

The study comes from years of struggling to have a consistent prayer life. I still struggle at times, but when I am at a loss as to how to pray or what to pray, I now go to the scriptures. I can find the words that are straight out of the bible.

I was first taught to pray scripture at an Aglow International women's group. The leader gave me a scripture and asked me to pray it aloud, putting it in my own words. I gave her a strange look and thought I don't know how to do this, but she encouraged me to try. She instructed me to put myself in the situation and exchange my name for the one in the scripture. Instead of David saying, "Help Lord" I could say "Help me Lord." I could say, "Thank You Lord that You come to my rescue."

I soon learned that I had all of scripture to use as my prayer book. The Psalms are for praise and making declarations of trust in the Lord. The books of Samuel, Kings and Chronicles teach me how to win a battle and how God dealt with His people. I can pray like David and Jehoshaphat calling on the Lord to defeat my enemies. The books of the prophets taught me to pray for our nation, the church, and Israel. The New Testament is filled with prayers for those who do not know God, for our families, the church of Jesus Christ. I discovered who I am in Christ and can pray for others to have that same relationship. I can now pull down the strongholds of the enemy who try to keep us from following after the Lord. I can decree and declare, "Thy kingdom come Thy will be done on earth as it is in heaven."

My prayer for those who study these lessons is that your prayer life will be exciting. I pray you will come to know how powerful your prayers are, even to the pulling down of enemy strongholds. I pray you will know the height and depth of God's great love for you.

Table of Contents

How to Pray and
Never Run Out of Words

Lesson 1

(All Scriptures are quoted from the New American Standard Version
unless otherwise noted. All homework is in bold italics print.)

A.) Your prayers are powerful.

Will we ever consistently pray unless we believe our
prayers are effective? When we realize that God does
hear our prayers and answers them, our faith will
grow. God is the one who commands us to pray while
He uses our prayers to break the enemy's grip on us.
God sends His Holy Spirit to us to teach us to pray
and then our wonderful God answers. The only thing
we have to do is obey His commands; He will do the
rest.

**<u>James 1:5,</u> "But if any of you lacks wisdom, let him
ask of God, who gives to all generously and
without reproach, and it will be given to him."**

I will never forget the day I discovered this verse, it
was one of my first prayers after I gave my life to the
Lord. I knew I lacked godly wisdom, and desperately
needed it. I was very unhappy and desired relief from
my circumstances, but I also wanted to know God's

will for my life. I knew God must have a better plan than mine.

God gives wisdom from above to all who earnestly seek Him. We should seek guidance from God's Word if our prayers are to be effective. In the following passage, Paul gives detailed instructions to a young pastor named Timothy.

<u>I Timothy 2: 1-8,</u> "First of all, then, I urge that entreaties and prayers, petitions and thanksgivings, be made on behalf of all men, for kings and all who are in authority, so that we may lead a tranquil and quiet life in all godliness and dignity. This is good and acceptable in the sight of God our Savior, who desires all men to be saved and to come to the knowledge of the truth. For there is one God, and one mediator also between God and men, the man Christ Jesus, who gave Himself as a ransom for all, the testimony given at the proper time. For this I was appointed a preacher and an apostle (I am telling the truth, I am not lying) as a teacher of the Gentiles in faith and truth. Therefore I want the men in every place to pray, lifting up holy hands, without wrath and dissension."

Timothy tells us God desires all to be saved. Since Jesus paid a very high price for us, by dying on the cross, shouldn't we desire to see Him have what He has paid for? All believers should pray, not just for their own families, but for the lost and for all who are in authority. This means the people in your neighborhood, the government in your town, religious leaders and even the homeless person on the street corner.

> - *Take a few minutes to pray for those in authority so you will lead a quiet and peaceable life. Write out your prayer.*

Lord God,

I pray protection, peace, safety,

and wisdom for the lost souls and

the ones in authority. In Jesus name, Amen.

B.) Prayer tears down enemy strongholds.

2 Corinthians 10: 3-4, "For though we walk in the flesh, we do not war according to the flesh, for the weapons of our warfare are not of the flesh, but divinely powerful for the destruction of fortresses."

Our greatest weapon is the word of God and we need to wield it against the enemy. Scripture is a powerful sword that cuts through the lies and reveals the truth. Tell the enemy of your soul what the Bible says about your circumstances.

Hebrews 4:12, "For the word of God is living and active and sharper than any two-edged sword, and piercing as far as the division of soul and spirit, of both joints and marrow, and able to judge the thoughts and intentions of the heart."

V. 4, (NKJV), "For the weapons of our warfare are not carnal but mighty in God for <u>pulling down stronghold**s.**</u>"

A stronghold is a fortress or a place of refuge. The Lord is our refuge and stronghold; we can run to Him and be safe. The devil builds up strongholds of a different type that are against the will of God. He lies and builds up strongholds in our minds that keep us from the truth of God.

The devil's strongholds are built on lies and deceit. If he can convince us that prayer is a waste of time or is boring, then we will never accomplish what God intends for us. When we are deceived, it is difficult for us to hear the truth of God's word.

- *Write out a list of the lies the devil has told you. Ask the Lord to show you how you have been robbed by the enemy.*

1. You're not smart enough

2. You're not worthy or good enough

3. Continue to worry + fear the future.

4

We need to change our thinking and reject the lies of the enemy. Satan will tell you that you don't matter and that your prayers will never make any difference in your community, your family, or your nation. God says differently:

James 5:16, "Is anyone among you sick? Then he must call for the elders of the church and they are to pray over him, anointing him with oil in the name of the Lord; and the prayer offered in faith will restore the one who is sick, and the Lord will raise him up, and if he has committed sins, they will be forgiven him. Therefore, confess your sins to one another, and pray for one another so that you may be healed. The effective prayer of a righteous man can accomplish much."

In this verse, James is instructing the church to pray because our prayers are effective. He especially mentions the sick in this passage and tells us *(the church)* to call for the elders of the church to pray. I have witnessed many healings and other answered prayers at the church altar.

- *Do you know of anyone healed after prayer? Write briefly about your experience.*

Drug Addicts who devote themselves to Christ & get sober.

James 5:17-18, "Elijah was a man with a nature like ours, and he prayed earnestly that it would not rain, and it did not rain on the earth for three years and six months. Then he prayed again, and the sky poured rain and the earth produced its fruit."

God will use ordinary people like you and me to change circumstances in our families, our communities and our nation. All we have to do is pray and obey. *(This is a recurring theme throughout scripture.)* We will reap the rewards of our prayers if we remain steadfast. Do not give up!

C.) It is God's will that we pray.

Isaiah 56:7, "Even those I will bring to My holy mountain and make them joyful in My house of prayer. Their burnt offerings and their sacrifices will be acceptable on My altar; for My house will be called a house of prayer for all the peoples."

Mark 11:17, "And He began to teach and say to them, "Is it not written, 'My house shall be called a house of prayer for all the nations?"

If we desire God's blessings in our lives, we must walk in God's will. In the Scriptures, He reveals His will for us.

We don't have to be giants of faith. Simply obey and trust God to do what He says He will do when we pray. Anything less, would be calling God a liar. *(Think about it.)*

✳ D.) Begin and end all prayer by recognizing who God is.

1.) Prayer and praise will flow naturally when we acknowledge God's character.

Isaiah 44:6, "I am the first and the last; there is no God besides Me."

Isaiah 44:8, "…Is there any God besides Me, or is there any other Rock? I know of none."

Psalms 24:7-9, Lift up your heads, O gates, and be lifted up, O ancient doors, that the King of glory may come in! Who is the King of glory? The Lord strong and mighty, The Lord mighty in battle. Lift up your heads, O gates, and lift them up, O ancient doors, That the King of glory may come in!

Jeremiah 10:6-8, "There is none like You, O Lord; You are great, and great is Your name in might. Who would not fear You, O King of the nations? Indeed it is Your due! For among all the wise men of the nations and in all their kingdoms, there is none like You."

When we recognize the King of Glory, the Lord most High all we are compelled to worship Him.

- *Write out what these scriptures mean to you personally.*

They praise & acknowledge God for all the wonderful things he does, and is, and continues to be.

2). The Lord of Lords deserves praise - thank Him ahead of time for answering your prayers.

Ps. 18:1-3, "I love the Lord, my strength. The Lord is my rock and my fortress and my deliverer, my God, my rock, in whom I take refuge; my shield and the horn of my salvation, my stronghold. I call upon the Lord, who is worthy to be praised. And I am saved from my enemies."

Write about how these facts can change your life.
Write out a prayer of thanks to the Lord for being
your shelter in time of trouble.

Lord,
Thank you for always being the one I
can run to & trust to take care
of me in both the good & bad
times. You are my shelter at all
times and especially in times of
trouble. Oh how much I love
you, LORD!

E.) Pray the scriptures and never run out of words.

<u>Hebrews 4:12</u> (King James Version), "For the word of God is quick, and powerful, and sharper than any two edged sword, piercing even to the dividing asunder of soul and spirit, and of the joints and marrow, and is a discerner of the thoughts and intents of the heart."

When we use the scriptures for prayer, we can be assured that we are in agreement with the Lord of Heaven and Earth, the All Mighty Lord of the Universe. Isn't that what we want when we pray? Our powerful, effective prayers will move heaven and earth. How exciting is that?

Pray the Word of God back to God. You will never run out of words – the Bible has endless resources.

Examples of prayers from the Scriptures:

1.) In trouble - **Ps. 61:1-4, Ps. 91** – Hear my cry, Oh Lord.

2.) Need forgiveness - **Ps. 51:10 -12**, and **1-4**, and **Ps.50: 14-15**, Create in me a clean heart.

3.) Pray for yourself or others – **Eph. 3:16-19**, Be filled with God.

4.) Pray for anyone who is hurting – **Ps 34:19, Is.54:4-5**, Fear not; He heals the broken hearted.

5.) When you need God to be your defense - **Ps. 37**, Take refuge in Him.

6.) Praise – **Ps 100, and 148,** Give thanks to the Lord – He is worthy.

- *Write your prayer back to God using these verses.*

Father God,

Create in me a clean heart, remove any wickedness or evil. Heal me of my selfishness, I take refuge in you and you are my defense. Bless me and fill me w/ your holy spirit Lord, Heal me from this sickness I

10 experience, Help me O Lord!

Amen.

F.) *Homework:*

- *Day 1)* **Read Isaiah 55 and write what you learn from God's free offer of mercy – notice there is a progression in our relationship with God:**

  a.) come be satisfied – verses 1-4

  _____

  _____

  b.) come repent – verses 5-7

  _____

  _____

  c.) come be transformed- verses 8-11

  _____

  _____

  d.) come and rejoice – verses 12-13

  _____

  _____

- *Day 2) Read 2 Chronicles 20:1-34, how to win a battle. This is one of the most exciting and historic battles in all of Bible history. Take note of the steps Jehoshaphat took.*

- *Day 3) Read 2 Chronicles 20:1-5 and answer the following questions:*

a.) What did Jehoshaphat do first?

_____

_____

_____

b.) Write out what he did next. Begin by writing sequential numbers in your Bible, marking each step Jehoshaphat and God take in this chapter.

_____

_____

_____

- *Day 4) 2 Chronicles 20:6-12 - What does he pray? Write out each step.*

a.) Write out what he says about God.

_____

_____

_____

b.) How does he state his case before the Lord?

_____

_____

_____

c.) How does he end his prayer?

_____

_____

_____

d.) He pours out his complaint. Do you have a
   complaint to pour out to the Lord? Write it
   out here:

_____

_____

_____

- *Day 5) 2 Chronicles 20:13 – 17, How*
   does God respond? Write what you have
   learned.

_____

_____

_____

V.18-19 Write out Jehoshaphat's response to
God.

_____

_____

_____

a.) Read the rest of this chapter and write out what you learned about how to win a battle. Observe how God deals with His people and how He deals with the enemy when His people pray.

_____

_____

_____

_____

Closing prayer:

Thank You Lord for all you are teaching me. I desire to pray the things that are on Your heart. Come Holy Spirit and teach me to pray and thank You that You are a God who answers prayer.

Have a wonderful week and remember the Lord loves you so much He sent His only Son to die for you. He paid the price you could never pay because of His great love for you.

How to Pray and Never Run Out of Words

Lesson 2

(All Scriptures are quoted from the New American Standard Version unless otherwise noted. All homework is in bold italics print.)

A. Communication with God

1.) Talk to Him because He loves us.

1 John 4:9-10, **"By this the love of God was manifested in us, that God has sent His only begotten Son into the world so that we might live through Him. In this is love, not that we loved God, but that He loved us and sent His Son to be the propitiation for our sins."**

God loves us so much that He not only saved us from our sins, but He desires fellowship (*companionship*) with us. The Lord of the Universe wishes to talk to us and to hear us talk back to Him.

2.) We should want to be with the One we love:

- When we love someone, we want to share our lives with them, our sorrows and our joys.

- We should care about them and their concerns and want to spend time with them.

- When we love someone, we form a true loving friendship built on two-way communication. We need to listen as well as talk. From the beginning in the garden, it was God's plan to walk and talk with us.

B. Will you allow Satan to win you over?

1.) Satan wants to separate us from God:

Genesis 3:8-9, **"They heard the sound of the Lord God walking in the garden in the cool of the day, and the man and his wife hid themselves from the presence of the Lord God among the trees of the garden. Then the Lord God called to the man, and said to him, "Where are you?" He said, "I heard the sound of You in the garden, and I was afraid because I was naked; so I hid myself."**

They recognized God's footsteps, so they must have known Him well. (*I recognize my husband's footsteps.*) Notice that shame entered the world in this verse. This is one of the tactics the enemy uses to stop us from moving ahead with the Lord. Shame will separate us from God and cause us to hide from Him.

2.) Satan tries to distract us:

In the book of John, Jesus rebuked religious Jews because they did not recognize Him as the Messiah, but were seeking to kill Him. The devil deceived them into thinking Jesus was a false prophet.

John 8:44, "You are of your father the devil, and you want to do the desires of your father. He was a murderer from the beginning, and does not stand in the truth because there is no truth in him. Whenever he speaks a lie, he speaks from his own nature, for he is a liar and the father of lies."

We must not allow the enemy to distract us from our relationship with the Lord. We can all be distracted and doubt God when we listen to Satan's lies. It is very important for us to recognize his tactics: deceit, fear, shame and bitterness (unforgiveness) are the enemy's weapons. They are based in lies.

We all have hiding places within us where our secret sin is buried. We would prefer to keep hiding it, but if we allow the Lord to shine His light into those places the enemy will be defeated. Satan flees from the light because he lives in darkness and deceit. When we allow the light of God's truth to shine on the hidden areas of our lives, the darkness flees and we are set free. *(They are not hidden from the Lord, anyway.)*

- *Write out some of the lies the enemy has told you.*

_____

_____

_____

C. How do we fight the enemy?

1.) Jesus fought with the Word of God:

The greatest example is how Jesus fought Satan. Jesus knew what the scriptures said and He spoke them to the enemy.

Matthew 4:3-4, "And the tempter came and said to Him, "If You are the Son of God, command that these stones become bread." But He answered and said, "It is written, 'Man shall not live on bread alone, but on every word that proceeds out of the mouth of God.'"

Matthew 4:10-11, "Then Jesus said to him, "Go, Satan! For it is written, 'You shall worship the Lord your God, and serve Him only.'" Then the devil left Him; and behold, angels came and began to minister to Him."

Learn to speak to the enemy what God says about your circumstances. Jesus quoted scripture to Satan and he fled – we have to fight smart like Jesus.

- ***Give an example of what you can tell the enemy in order to defeat him.***

_____

_____

_____

_____

We don't have to quote the Bible perfectly, but we do need to understand what God says about our situation. You can ask your pastor or a trust worthy Christian counselor for guidance helping you to find what the scripture says about your situation. Then during the day as the enemy attacks you with negative thoughts practice telling the enemy what God says about your circumstances.

Just as armies do not go into battle without being trained, we must also learn the enemies' tactics, weaknesses and strengths in order to defeat them. Are you ill? God is your Healer. Are you afraid? God is trustworthy. Are you in need? God is your provider, etc. We need to practice praying what God has to say about our situations.

- *What are Satan's weapons?*

_____

_____

_____

- *What is our greatest weapon?*

_____

_____

_____

2.) Our spiritual weapons:

Ephesians 6:10-17, **"Therefore, take up the full armor of God, so that you will be able to resist in the evil day, and having done everything, to stand firm. Stand firm therefore, having girded your loins with truth, and having put on the breastplate of righteousness, and having shod your feet with the preparation of the gospel of peace; in addition to all, taking up the shield of faith with which you will be able to extinguish all the flaming arrows of the evil one. And take the helmet of salvation, and the sword of the Spirit, which is the word of God."**

Ephesians 6: 18, **"With all prayer and petition pray at all times in the Spirit, and with this in**

view, be on the alert with all perseverance and petition for all the saints,…"

Jesus clothes us with His armor when we accept Him as Lord and Savior. We do not take it off at night like we remove our clothing, although it is good to remind ourselves often that we are clothed with God's armor. We have protective armor, our shield of faith and helmet of salvation, we have truth, righteousness and peace. Notice, our offensive weapon, the sword of the Spirit is the word of God. Paul admonishes us to put on the armor of God, and then he tells us to pray with all types of prayer and petition, at all times, in the Spirit.

(I repeat the scripture below, because we need to embrace it as part of our DNA; get it down in our spirit.)

<u>2 Corinthians 10:3,</u> " …**For though we walk in the flesh, we do not war according to the flesh,…"**

The Word of God (*Scripture*) is described as a spiritual weapon of great power. The sword of the Spirit cuts straight to the heart of things. It cuts past excuses and defenses and confronts us with the truth. Example: We say, "I can't," but God says, "My grace is sufficient for you." You say, "I am weak," but God says, "I have given you a spirit of power." There are multiples of examples in the scriptures. Learn what God has to say.

2 Timothy 1:7, "For God has not given us a spirit of fear, but of power and of love and of a sound mind."

- *Write out a prayer, saying what the Lord has to say about your situation, and then tell the devil what God has to say about it.*

_____

_____

_____

D. Approaching God

1.) When we approach God it should be in reverence:

Hebrews 10:22, "...let us draw near with a sincere heart in full assurance of faith, having our hearts sprinkled clean from an evil conscience and our bodies washed with pure water."

James 4:8, "Draw near to God and He will draw near to you. Cleanse your hands, you sinners; and purify your hearts, you double-minded."

When we come before the Lord, we need to ask Him to cleanse us from our sins. Sin separates us from God, not because He has abandoned us, but because we have broken the relationship with Him. We are still His children; however, our sin causes us to pull away from God. To repair the relationship we need to confess and repent of our wrong doings. The Lord is faithful to forgive us; the shed blood of Jesus Christ cleanses us. As we turn from our sin, we can approach God without guilt or shame, with nothing between us.

Psalms 139:23-24, "Search me, O God, and know my heart; try me and know my anxious thoughts; and see if there be any hurtful way in me, and lead me in the everlasting way."

Proverbs 14:26-27, "In the fear of the Lord there is strong confidence, and his children will have refuge. The fear of the Lord is a fountain of life, that one may avoid the snares of death."

The bible tells us to reverence and fear the Lord so that we will avoid the snares of death. Our prayers are hindered by sin and unrepentance, but God Himself protects us when we ask forgiveness, for He has made a way for us to receive newness of life. As we sincerely ask His pardon, He will be faithful to forgive.

2.) Jesus taught us how to pray:

Matthew 6: 7-15, "…And when you are praying, do not use meaningless repetition as the Gentiles do, for they suppose that they will be heard for their many words. So do not be like them; for your Father knows what you need before you ask Him. "Pray, then, in this way: 'Our Father who is in heaven, Hallowed be Your name. 'Your kingdom come. Your will be done, on earth as it is in heaven. 'Give us this day our daily bread. 'And forgive us our debts, as we also have forgiven our debtors. 'And do not lead us into temptation, but deliver us from evil. [For Yours is the kingdom and the power and the glory forever. Amen.'] For if you forgive others for their transgressions, your heavenly Father will also forgive you. But if you do not forgive others, then your Father will not forgive your transgressions."

Begin by recognizing who God is and what He has done for you, **V. 9**. He is our Father in Heaven. We communicate with the Lord on many levels. He is the Holy Lord of All, our Savior, Redeemer, and Shepherd, Ruler of the Universe, our Faithful Friend and so much more.

We should always desire that His will be done and that He is glorified on earth as He is in heaven, **V.10**. Think about your motives for prayer. Do you desire God's glory or just relief from your problems?

V. 8, 11, God directs us to tell Him all our needs, even though He knows them anyway.

V.12-13, God instructs us to repent, ask forgiveness of our sins, and ask Him to keep us from temptation.

V. 14-15, God makes it very clear that if we don't forgive others, the Lord will not forgive us. Isn't that a scary thought? He has done so much for us and desires us to be completely free from bitterness and unforgiveness. At the cross, Jesus paid the same price for those who have wounded us as He paid for us. If we love Him, we should desire that He receives all those He paid for on Calvary.

E. Pray without Ceasing

1.) Never give up:

<u>I Thessalonians 5:17-18</u>, tells us to "… **pray without ceasing; in everything give thanks; for this is God's will for you in Christ Jesus.**"

How can we pray without ceasing? Pray in the Spirit throughout the day by being aware of God's presence at all times. Pray when getting dressed in the morning; bless your family as they leave for the day. Pray for our country when you hear the news, pray in the car or while you are fixing dinner, and pray at bedtime. I believe you get the idea; praying without ceasing is a matter of practicing prayer as a way of life.

2.) When we are weak, He is strong:

Romans 8:26, **"In the same way the Spirit also helps our weakness; for we do not know how to pray as we should, but the Spirit Himself intercedes for us with groanings too deep for words; …"**

When you are unsure of what to pray, ask the Holy Spirit to direct you. Then pray until you have a sense of direction from God. You can also just spend some time reading the Psalms. They are the greatest prayers ever written and are intended to be a prayer book.

- *Pray Psalms 146:1-6 to the Lord in your own words. Write your prayer down.*

_____

_____

_____

_____

_____

_____

F. There are so many types of prayer in Scripture - you will never run out of words.

1.) Prayer is communicating with God. A few types of prayer are: Praise and worship, petition, spiritual warfare, making declarations of who God is and what he has done, praying the scriptures and telling the enemy what God has to say about your situation

- *Write out all the types of prayer you personally use.*

_____

_____

_____

1.) Praise is a powerful weapon:

Praise is defined in Webster's dictionary as a verb; meaning to extol or glorify. As illustrated throughout the Psalms, King David knew how to praise the Lord. Shouldn't we, also, praise the Lord at all times?

Psalms 34:1-3, "**I will bless the Lord at all times; His praise shall continually be in my mouth. My soul will make its boast in the Lord; The humble**

**will hear it and rejoice. O magnify the Lord with
me, And let us exalt His name together."**

Moses wrote:
Exodus 15:11, **"Who is like You among the gods, O
Lord? Who is like You, majestic in holiness,
Awesome in praises, working wonders?"**

After many years of enslavement, God delivered His
people out of Egypt safely and not one was lame or
sick. After they crossed the Red Sea their natural
response was to praise the Lord. Moses' sister,
Miriam, took out her tambourine as the people
rejoiced.

Exodus 15:1-2, **"Then Moses and the sons of Israel
sang this song to the Lord, and said, "I will sing to
the Lord, for He is highly exalted; the horse and its
rider He has hurled into the sea. "The Lord is my
strength and song, and He has become my
salvation; this is my God, and I will praise Him;
My father's God, and I will extol Him."**

How much more should we praise the Lord for all He
has done for us? He has given us salvation, healing,
deliverance, as well as the great privilege of entering
into His presence and having Him reside within us.
Wow, what a wonderful God!

Psalms 92:1-4, **" It is good to give thanks to the
Lord And to sing praises to Your name, O Most**

High; To declare Your lovingkindness in the morning and Your faithfulness by night, with the ten-stringed lute and with the harp, with resounding music upon the lyre. For You, O Lord, have made me glad by what You have done, I will sing for joy at the works of Your hands."

- *Write out a prayer of praise in your own words from Psalm 92.*

_____

_____

_____

_____

_____

_____

_____

_____

Homework:

- **Day 1)** Write out a prayer asking the Lord to teach you to pray and to direct your prayers according to His will.

_____

_____

_____

- **Day 2)** Write out what God would say to Satan about your struggles.

_____

_____

_____

- **Day 3)** List some of the prayers God has answered for you and spend a few minutes praising Him for His faithfulness.

_____

_____

_____

- ***Day 4)*** *Write out a few prayer requests that you are still waiting for God to answer. Praise the Lord for His working in these situations. Thank God for His faithfulness.*

_____

_____

_____

_____

- ***Day 5)*** *Read and pray* **Psalm 91** *to the Lord. Write down the parts that especially encourage you.*

_____

_____

_____

_____

Do not be discouraged - the enemy does not want you to learn to pray. He knows the power of your prayers and he fears you. Have a wonderful week and I promise, if you do the homework, the Lord will bless you abundantly as you spend time with Him.

How to Pray and Never Run Out of Words

Lesson 3

(All Scriptures are from the New American Standard Version unless otherwise noted. All homework is in bold italics print.)

A. Prayer of Petition

1.) Keep on asking:

The prayer of petition is one of the most common types of prayer. We all have needs, whether we are young or old, rich or poor, healthy or ill – we have needs only God can provide. Our petitions may vary, but our requests for personal needs, our spouses, children, family and our friends remain similar.

A petition is a formal request, directed to a deity or a superior. It is an application to a court for a writ, or judicial action in a lawsuit. It can also be a written application signed by many people appealing to higher authority. When we pray, we petition the Lord for our needs.

The Lord is our Higher Authority, He listens attentively to our petitions. The scripture tells us to make our requests known to Him. God knows what we need and want, but desires to use us in the process of bringing about the answers. The scriptures are filled with prayers of praise and petition. Here is an example:

Psalms 146:1-5, "Praise the Lord! Praise the Lord, O my soul! I will praise the Lord while I live; I will sing praises to my God while I have my being. Do not trust in princes, in mortal man, in whom there is no salvation. His spirit departs, he returns to the earth; in that very day his thoughts perish. How blessed is he whose help is the God of Jacob, Whose hope is in the Lord his God..."

- *Take time to pray these verses back to God.*

_____

_____

_____

_____

_____

_____

_____

Let the Lord direct you:

Learn how to use the many prayers found in the scriptures, offering petitions for the church, the nation and the things that are on God's heart. If you have never asked God what is on His heart – try it. You can use the scripture below:

I Thessalonians 3:11-13, "Now may our God and Father Himself and Jesus our Lord direct our way to you; and may the Lord cause you to increase and abound in love for one another, and for all people, just as we also do for you; so that He may establish your hearts without blame in holiness before our God and Father at the coming of our Lord Jesus with all His saints."

When there is turmoil in your life or within your family, turn to the Lord so that you may abound in His love. In the following verse, place the pronouns with the person's name that is the object of your prayers.

Ephesians 4:16-19, "…that He would grant you, (_____) according to the riches of His glory, to be strengthened with power through His Spirit in the inner man, so that Christ may dwell in your hearts through faith; and that you, being rooted and grounded in love, may be able to comprehend with all the saints what is the breadth and length

and height and depth, and to know the love of Christ which surpasses knowledge, that you may be filled up to all the fullness of God."

I like to pray this especially for the men in my life; however, you can apply it to anyone. Remember, your prayers are powerful and when you pray the Scriptures, you can be assured that you are praying a powerful prayer.

- *Put Ephesians 4:16-19 into your own words and pray it back to the Lord. Write out your prayer.*

_____

_____

_____

_____

3.) You have a call to prayer from God:

Intercessory prayer is the simple act of praying for someone else. We may get nervous or fell unsure if someone talks about intercessory prayer. We may think, "I'm not called to that," but we are all called to intercede. When we pray for someone else – we are practicing intercessory prayer. Rather, Christians wield spiritual weaponry that is far more powerful than any human device.

In the bible, God directs us to pray not only for ourselves, but also for others, for spiritual leaders, government leaders, and even for the nations. He tells us to bless Israel and to pray for the peace of Jerusalem. God promises to bless those who bless Israel and to curse those who come against Israel.

The moment you accept Jesus Christ as your Savior, you become the enemy of God's enemies. Like it or not, you have an enemy and God gives you the privilege of taking authority over him. You don't have to be fearful – God is on your side. Joni Erickson Toda, Christian author, used to say, "God and me make a majority."

The Lord hears our prayer and then He fights the battle for us. Our job is to pray and obey, and then praise the Lord for His answers. We can praise Him before the answer comes because we know God is the Mighty Warrior, King Eternal, the Almighty God. Praise Him because He hears our prayers and is working on our behalf. Then when prayers are answered we praise Him again for what He has done for us.

I Timothy 2:1-2, "First of all, then, I urge that entreaties and prayers, petitions and thanksgivings, be made on behalf of all men, ..."

We pray for "all" because the Lord commands it and we should obey Him. Our nation will be changed if God's people diligently pray for our pastors and political leaders. I truly believe the church can turn the tide of ungodliness in this nation. He is giving us grace and opportunity to turn our country back to Him, for His glory. I don't see any place in scripture where it tells us "what will be, will be". No, He says "pray and trust".

4.) There is hope:

II Chronicles 7:13-15, **"If I shut up the heavens so that there is no rain, or if I command the locust to devour the land, or if I send pestilence among My people, and My people who are called by My name humble themselves and pray and seek My face and turn from their wicked ways, then I will hear from heaven, will forgive their sin and will heal their land. Now My eyes will be open and My ears attentive to the prayer offered in this place."**

This scripture may be familiar, but do we truly believe that God means what He says and will act upon it? Our nation is certainly in a spiritual drought and many churches are dried up and dying. A pestilence has come upon our land. Hatred and violence seem to be devouring many people, **BUT God is still answering the prayers of the saints,** if we will take heed, turn from our wicked ways and pray. Never let the lies of the enemy tell you that it's too late or that your prayers don't matter.

Are you discouraged? Do you think it is too late for America to turn back to God? These are the lies of the enemy. God is calling us to take a stand, to rise up and tell the enemy what He has to say about our land.

Christian men and women who dedicated our government to Godly principles founded this nation. They weren't perfect men, but they recognized that if God was not in the establishment of our constitution and laws this nation would not endure. No other nation in all of history began in such a manner. God, Himself, established Israel; men, established the United States, in God's name, for His glory.

- **We can pray in Jesus name:** *Lord, do not let any forces of hell take from You what was dedicated to You from the beginning. Don't let the peoples say there is no God in America. Be glorified in this land; let Your kingdom come and Your will be done. Lord, be high and lifted up and let the light of Your glory be seen across the face of this nation.*

Psalms 61:1-4, "Hear my cry, O God; Give heed to my prayer. From the end of the earth I call to You when my heart is faint; lead me to the rock that is higher than I. For You have been a refuge for me, a tower of strength against the enemy. Let me

dwell in Your tent forever; Let me take refuge in the shelter of Your wings."

In nature, God gives us a beautiful picture of mother hens sheltering their babies under their wings. Swans glide across the waters with a dozen babies kept safely on their backs, under their wings. This is a reflection of how God covers us.

The Lord is my shelter and when I am in trouble or discouraged I can hide under His wings. I can run to Him for protection in the storms of life and we glide over the troubled waters together. The more I learn about the Lord, the easier it is to put my trust in Him.

B. Devoted To Prayer

1.) The power is in prayer:

As a young Christian, I desired the gift of healing. To lay hands on people and see them healed seemed so exciting, and it still does, but now I realize the real power is in prayer. The gifts of healing and miracles are the natural overflow of prayer.

Luke 6: 12, "It was at this time that He (*Jesus*) went off to the mountain to pray, and He spent the whole night in prayer to God."

If Jesus felt the need to pray all night, how much more should we see the need for prayer in our lives? Jesus is our example of how to live a Christian life and while on earth, He submitted Himself fully to the Father. A very large part of God's plan for us is to partner with Him in tearing down enemy strongholds in prayer.

Luke 18:1, "Now He was telling them a parable to show that at all times they ought to pray and not to lose heart. "

Matthew 7:7-8, "Ask, and it will be given to you; seek, and you will find; knock, and it will be opened to you. For everyone who asks receives, and he who seeks finds, and to him who knocks it will be opened."

God repeats Himself and so will I. Don't ever give up or give in to discouragement. Pray fervently, don't give up until your prayers are answered.

These verbs, ask, seek and knock translate in Greek, to keep on asking, keep on seeking and keep on knocking. Do not ever, ever give up.

The lies of the enemy will stop us from receiving what God has for us. Remember that lies are the enemy's only weapon. He tries to convince us that God doesn't hear or does not care. He tells us, "Don't bother to pray, you have no power, you will never see this prayer answered." Do any of these lies sound familiar?

Scientists say the night is darkest just before dawn. Sometimes, situations in our lives get worse before they get better. One of my family members wound up in jail before he heard the Lord's call on his life. His Mom never stopped praying for him. God saved him in prison and delivered him from all the hurts in his life. Now God uses him mightily to share the gospel as well as giving hope for the future to those who are incarcerated.

Many of us may be experiencing dark times, but this is definitely not the time to stop praying. Cling to the Lord, vow to **never** give up. Tell the enemy that he won't win this battle because God is on your side. Tell him he has no authority over you and your family because you belong to the Lord Almighty and you have dedicated yourself and your family to Him.

2.) Devote yourself to pray:

Acts 1:14, (the apostles) **"These all with one mind were continually devoting themselves to prayer, along with the women, and Mary the mother of Jesus, and with His brothers."**

The disciples knew it was important to devote themselves to prayer. Shouldn't we, as disciples of Christ, devote ourselves to prayer? Scripture goes on to say that on the day of Pentecost, they were all together in the upper room. The Lord baptized them with the Holy Spirit and with the evidence of speaking in tongues. Today there is still power in the prayer of agreement; this is why we join together to pray. Agreeing with one another encourages us and discourages the enemy.

Acts 2: 1-4, "**And when the day of Pentecost had come, they were all together in one place. And suddenly there came from heaven a noise like a violent rushing wind, and it filled the whole house where they were sitting. And there appeared to them tongues as of fire distributing themselves, and they rested on each one of them. And they were all filled with the Holy Spirit and began to speak with other tongues, as the Spirit was giving them utterance.**"

The Baptism of the Holy Spirit gives us power to witness to others and power in our prayers. The disciples were frightened and hiding before they received the Baptism of the Holy Spirit, but afterwards they shared the gospel with boldness. The book of Acts is filled with examples of the believers' acts of daring with miracles following. When they stood in Jewish synagogues and preached Jesus, they healed the sick and were accused of turning the world upside down.

We receive the Baptism of the Holy Spirit by faith, just as we received salvation. It is God's desire for us. The Baptism of the Holy Spirit is a free gift of God and He will give it freely to those who ask of Him.

Don't forget what Paul tells us about praying in the Spirit.

Romans 8:26, "In the same way the Spirit also helps our weakness; for we do not know how to pray as we should, but the Spirit Himself intercedes for us with groanings too deep for words; …"

Acts 1:8, "but you will receive power when the Holy Spirit has come upon you; and you shall be My witnesses both in Jerusalem, and in all Judea and Samaria, and even to the remotest part of the earth."

God gives us extraordinary gifts in order to equip us for ministry. These scriptures show us two powerful purposes, power in prayer and power to witness. The book of Acts gives us several examples of people being saved and then filled with the Baptism of the Holy Spirit, with the evidence of speaking in tongues.

4.) We are all called to be witnesses to the lost and to pray at all times.

Isaiah 44:3-5, "For I will pour out water on the thirsty land and streams on the dry ground; I will pour out My Spirit on your offspring and My blessing on your descendants; and they will spring up among the grass like poplars by streams of water. "This one will say, 'I am the Lord's'; and

that one will call on the name of Jacob; and another will write on his hand, 'Belonging to the Lord,' and will name Israel's name with honor."

- *Pray Isaiah's words back to the Lord: Lord, this land is dry and needs Your living waters to revive it. Pour out Your Holy Spirit on my offspring and me; let Your blessings pour out on my descendents. Let them grow and flourish in the knowledge of God, that they will be spiritually healthy as a green tree planted by the streams of water. I ask that they would mature and bring forth the Fruit of the Spirit, able to feed many others around them. Let them declare for all to hear, "I belong to the Lord; His name is written on my heart."*

- *Now you try it; write out your prayer:*

_____

_____

_____

_____

_____

_____

Homework:

- **Day 1)** *Pray <u>Isaiah 48:3-5</u> back to the Lord. We are spiritual Israel, grafted into the vine by Jesus. Our nation is certainly dry ground. We need God's Spirit poured out on the U.S.A. Substitute America for Israel and pray this back to the Lord. Write out your prayer.*

_____

_____

_____

_____

_____

- **Day 2)** *Pray 10 minutes for your family and for this nation. God cares deeply about both. Ask the Lord to touch your heart with the things that concern Him.*

- **Day 3)** *Read Ephesians 2: 1-22, it talks about who you are in Christ. Who are you?*

_____

_____

_____

_____

- **Day 4)** *Spend 15 minutes praising the Lord for who you are in Christ from Ephesians. Write out your praise (This will build your faith).*

_____

_____

_____

- **Day 5)** *Spend 10 minutes praying for others doing this study.*

May the Lord give you grace for each new challenge you face. May He give you favor in your family, your work place and in the community, just as you have favor with God in heaven.

How to Pray and Never Run Out of Words

Lesson 4

(All Scriptures are quoted from the New American Standard Version unless otherwise noted. All homework is in bold italics print.)

A. I will put my trust in You Lord.

1.) Trust and believe He will do what He says He will do:

How can we expect our prayers to be answered unless we trust the Lord? He loves us so much that He went to the cross for our sins, so we know by reading His word that He still loves us and wants what is good for us. If we don't believe that the Lord is true to His word, we are in big trouble.

Numbers 23:19, "God is not a man, that He should lie, nor a son of man, that He should repent; Has He said, and will He not do it? Or has He spoken, and will He not make it good?"

2.) He is the same yesterday, today, and forever:

Hebrews 13:8, "Jesus Christ is the same yesterday, today, and forever."

God does not change His mind about His promises. He has told us He is Jehovah-Rapha our healer, Jehovah-Jireh our provider, Jehovah-Shalom, our peace, Jehovah-Nissi, the Lord my banner or protector. These are just a few of the names the Lord calls Himself in scripture.

Psalms 31:1-5, "In You, O Lord, I have taken refuge; Let me never be ashamed; in Your righteousness deliver me. 2 Incline Your ear to me, rescue me quickly; be to me a rock of strength, a stronghold to save me. 3 For You are my rock and my fortress; for Your name's sake You will lead me and guide me. 4 You will pull me out of the net which they have secretly laid for me, for You are my strength. 5 Into Your hand I commit my spirit; You have ransomed me, O Lord, God of truth."

Psalms 31:14-16, "But as for me, I trust in You, O LORD, I say, "You are my God." [15] My times are in Your hand; Deliver me from the hand of my enemies and from those who persecute me. [16] Make Your face to shine upon Your servant; Save me in Your lovingkindness."

> *Read and pray all of Psalm 31 back to God in*
> *your own words.*

3.) Faith and trust are the same:

Without faith, trusting God is impossible. Without faith, we won't have peace or joy within, or be able to pray believing God will answer.

Hebrews 11:6, "And without faith it is impossible to please *Him*, for he who comes to God must believe that He is and *that* He is a rewarder of those who seek Him."

Proverbs 3:5, "Trust in the Lord with all your heart and do not lean on your own understanding."

We must have faith that we will see answers to our petitions. Pray and trust in Him, He will answer.

B. Pray that the Lord is glorified.

1.) How did Jesus pray?

Luke 22:41- 42, "And He withdrew from them about a stone's throw, and He knelt down and began to pray, saying, "Father, if You are willing, remove this cup from Me; yet not My will, but Yours be done."

Jesus prayed that the Father's will be done. Even though He knew He would go to the cross; Jesus laid down His will in exchange for the Father's desires. We should always surrender our will to God and desire to see Him glorified.

We may pray for the things that will comfort us or make us look good to others. For example, I could have just wanted God to release my family member from prison because of my embarrassment and so people would not think ill of my family. However, I wanted to see the Lord glorified through him more than I wanted his discharge.

I remember the prophetic words spoken over him as a child, so I prayed and agreed with the Lord that those prophetic words would come to pass. He is now out of prison and working with prison reform ministries. God is using him for His glory.

I Corinthians 10:31, "Whether, then, you eat or drink or whatever you do, do all to the glory of God."

He is worthy of all glory and all of our praise. Let us continually ask that God be glorified in this nation, in our families and in our churches.

Jude 24-25, "Now to Him who is able to keep you from stumbling, and to make you stand in the presence of His glory blameless with great joy, 25 to the only God our Savior, through Jesus Christ our Lord, be glory, majesty, dominion and authority, before all time and now and forever. Amen."

These verses from Jude tell us how we should feel about prayer, that the Lord be glorified now and forever. If we have a child who wants to please us or bless us, would we be inclined to grant that child favors? Of course, we would.

Remember what the Lord's Prayer tells us in **Matthew 6:10 , 13b, "Your kingdom come. Your will be done, on earth as it is in heaven. ... For Yours is the kingdom and the power and the glory forever. Amen."**

Psalms 79: 8-10a, "Do not remember the iniquities of our forefathers against us; let Your compassion come quickly to meet us, for we are brought very low. [9] Help us, O God of our salvation, for the glory of Your name; and deliver us and forgive our sins for Your name's sake. Why should the nations say, "Where is their God?"

Can you relate, as the psalmist did, to being brought low? The psalmist is in trouble; as a result, he calls on God and prays for the Lord to be glorified. Often when praying for a cancer patient or a situation where a person's life is being destroyed, I ask the Lord this question: "What glory is there for You in this untimely death? What glory is there for You, Lord, in a life that is destroyed by drugs or other sin?" I pray, "Lord be glorified."

- *Take a few moments and pray this scripture back to God with our nation in mind. Write out your prayer.*

_____

_____

_____

_____

C. What happens when prayer goes unanswered?

1.) We learn to trust:

We pray; we do what we believe the Lord desires and still things don't turn out like we thought they would. What do we do when we are disillusioned? How can we keep on trusting the Lord in the face of such disappointment?

This next scripture sounds like the prophet Habakkuk was discouraged because His prayers were not answered in the way he desired. In Habakkuk's time , things were similar to what we see happening in our society today.

Habakkuk 1:2-4, "How long, O Lord, will I call for help, and You will not hear? I cry out to You,

"Violence!" Yet You do not save. Why do You make me see iniquity, and cause me to look on wickedness? Yes, destruction and violence are before me; strife exists and contention arises. Therefore the law is ignored and justice is never upheld. For the wicked surround the righteous, therefore justice comes out perverted."

Habakkuk 1:13, "Your eyes are too pure to approve evil, and You cannot look on wickedness with favor. Why do You look with favor on those who deal treacherously? Why are You silent when the wicked swallow up those more righteous than they?"

- *Have you ever been in a similar situation in the past? Are you there now? Write out what you should do when you do not understand and don't know why things happen the way they do.*

_____

_____

_____

_____

Habakkuk 2:4, "Behold, as for the proud one, his soul is not right within him; but the righteous will live by his faith."

Habakkuk knew what it was like to trust, even when the enemy was about to overtake the land of Judah. To walk by faith is not always easy, but it is the only way to please the Lord. We need to make a lifelong decision to trust God, it is our only option.

The notes in my study bibles put it this way, "Faith, to Habakkuk, is even more than humble trust – it is faithfulness, the steadfast obedience to God which marks the life of faith. Faith is not just some doctrine which is believed – it is a whole way of life. It is daily dependence on God, walking with Him moment by moment."

Habakkuk 3:16, "I heard and my inward parts trembled, at the sound my lips quivered. Decay enters my bones, and in my place I tremble. Because I must wait quietly for the day of distress, for the people to arise who will invade us."

Habakkuk 3:17-19, "Though the fig tree should not blossom and there be no fruit on the vines, though the yield of the olive should fail And the fields produce no food, though the flock should be cut off from the fold and there be no cattle in the stalls, yet I will exult in the Lord, I will rejoice in the God of my salvation. The Lord God is my

strength (personnel bravery)**, and He has made my feet like hinds' feet, and makes me walk on my high places."**

This is one of my favorite passages in Scripture. When I am discouraged or confused, when things have not turned out the way I thought they should, I return to this passage. When the fig tree does not blossom and there is no fruit on the vines, it is then I renew my decision to trust the Lord. When my whole life seems to be falling apart, (*It has happened more than I would want to tell you)* I will trust in the Lord. He is the God who gives me strength and He will make me walk on the high places above the trials of life.

Job 13:15a, "Though He slay me, I will hope in Him."

Habakkuk 3:18, "Yet I will exalt in the Lord and rejoice in the God of my salvation."

I often pray, "Though my prayers are not answered, still I will put my trust in You. When my heart feels like it's breaking, I pray like Job. Although my prayers are not answered, still I will hope in You, Lord. I pray like Habakkuk, I will rejoice in You Lord."

When you exalt in the Lord He will give you personal bravery. He will make you to walk on the high places, above your circumstances. God becomes your strength it is not dependent the conditions you are living in. Praise the Lord, because He is worthy.

2.) When in turmoil we go back to the character traits of God. He is good:

Isaiah 55:8-9, "For My thoughts are not your thoughts, nor are your ways My ways," declares the Lord. "For as the heavens are higher than the earth, so are My ways higher than your ways and My thoughts than your thoughts."

The Lord tells us plainly that His thoughts are far above ours. He sees the full picture and we do not. We think we know what is best, but we do not. When we don't know why things happen the way they do, we need to put our trust in the Lord, for He is good. He is full of loving kindness and mercy. He showed us how He felt about us on the cross.

Psalm 31:19, "How great is Your goodness, which You have stored up for those who fear You, which You have wrought for those who take refuge in You, before the sons of men!"

Repeatedly in the Psalms it mentions the goodness, faithfulness and mercy of God. Read them often and meditate on the truths that God reveals to you. They will encourage and strengthen you in your daily walk with the Lord.

Exodus 33: 18-19, "Then Moses said, 'I pray You, show me Your glory!' And He said, 'I Myself will make all My goodness pass before you, and will proclaim the name of the Lord before you; and I will be gracious to whom I will be gracious, and will show compassion on whom I will show compassion.'"

In the book of Exodus, Moses is on the mountain having a conversation with the Lord when he asks God to show him His glory. The Lord could have revealed Himself in many ways. He might have made His power or majesty, His beauty or holiness known to Moses, but God chose to show him His goodness.

Exodus 33:21-22, "Then the Lord said, "Behold, there is a place by Me, and you shall stand there on the rock; and it will come about, while My glory is passing by, that I will put you in the cleft of the rock and cover you with My hand until I have passed by."

Three verses later the Lord says, that His glory will pass by. This illustrates to us His goodness and His glory are the same.

- *Think about the fact that now we have the Living God within us. He is not outside passing by anymore, but He is in us and we are in Him. Spend a few minutes thinking*

about what that means to you personally.
Write out your thoughts.

_____

_____

_____

_____

_____

_____

_____

_____

3.) The Lord is Sovereign – He gets the final say in our lives:

I Timothy 6: 15b-16 " **…He who is the blessed and only Sovereign, the King of kings and Lord of Lords, who alone possesses immortality and dwells in unapproachable light, whom no man has seen or can see. To Him be honor and eternal dominion! Amen.**"

Psalms 103:19, "The Lord has established His throne in the heavens, and His sovereignty rules over all."

The Lord is not obligated to tell us why things happen. He rules with loving kindness and mercy, moreover He asks us to trust Him.

4.) Praise is a weapon against the enemy:

Our greatest weapon against discouragement is praise. The enemy flees when we praise God. Praise the Lord even when you don't "feel" like it. I truly believe the enemy cannot stand to hear us worship the Lord.

Psalms 34:1-3, "I will bless the Lord at all times; His praise shall continually be in my mouth. My soul will make its boast in the Lord; the humble will hear it and rejoice. O magnify the Lord with me, and let us exalt His name together. I sought the Lord, and He answered me, and delivered me from all my fears."

When David wrote this Psalm, he was being chased all over the desert and was in fear for his life. He found solace and refuge in praising the Lord.

Psalms 32: 10-11, "Many are the sorrows of the wicked, But he who trusts in the Lord, lovingkindness shall surround him. Be glad in the Lord and rejoice, you righteous ones; and shout for joy, all you who are upright in heart."

David knew how to fight the enemy. The Lord made him a mighty warrior in the natural and the spiritual.

Homework:

- ***Day 1)*** *Read Psalms 103:1-22 and pray it back to the Lord. Write out your prayer – I promise you will be blessed.*

_____

_____

_____

_____

_____

_____

_____

- **_Day 2)_** _Write out a prayer asking the Lord to glorify Himself in your family._

_____

_____

_____

_____

_____

- **_Day 3)_** _Read <u>Psalms 138:1-8.</u> Write out a prayer giving thanks to the Lord for his favor._

_____

_____

_____

_____

_____

- *Day 4)* Pray for mercy and help for Israel and America referring to <u>Isaiah 64:1-4</u>. Write out your prayer.

_____

_____

_____

_____

_____

- *Day 5)* Spend 10 minutes just sitting and praising the Lord. Then spend 5 minutes being quiet and listening to the Lord. Write down what He places on your heart.

_____

_____

_____

_____

Have a wonderful week – praise the Lord all during your days, when you wake up and when you go to sleep. Just try it for one week; you'll see what a difference it will make in how you feel.

How to Pray and Never Run Out of Words

Lesson 5

(All Scriptures are quoted from the New American Standard Version unless otherwise noted. All homework is in bold italics print.)

A. Ask the Lord to cleanse your heart.

Before we enter into battle, we need to ask the Lord to cleanse us from all wrong motives and sin in our lives. Repentance and prayer go together. Don't give the enemy an inroad into your life through unforgiveness or besetting sin that will hinder your prayers.

Psalms 51:6-7, "Behold, You desire truth in the innermost being, and in the hidden part You will make me know wisdom. Purify me with hyssop, and I shall be clean; wash me, and I shall be whiter than snow."

Psalms 51:10-12, "Create in me a clean heart, O God, and renew a steadfast spirit within me. Do not cast me away from Your presence and do not take Your Holy Spirit from me. Restore to me the joy of Your salvation and sustain me with a willing spirit."

Ask the Lord to show you the sin in your life. Don't be afraid, the Lord loves you; He is gentle and will give you grace to repent. God will flood you with peace when you make the decision to surrender to Him.

- *Write out a prayer asking the Lord to cleanse your heart. If there is any unforgiveness in you, confess it. Moreover, make a decision to forgive and leave that person to the Lord. (He paid the same price for them as He did for you.) Ask Him to give you a heart that follows hard after Him.*

B. Warfare

1.) Our weapons:

Ephesians 6:16-18, "…in addition to all, taking up the shield of faith with which you will be able to extinguish all the flaming arrows of the evil one. And take the helmet of salvation, and the sword of the Spirit, which is the word of God. With all prayer and petition pray at all times in the Spirit, and with this in view, be on the alert with all perseverance and petition for all the saints…"

Hebrews 4:12, "For the word of God is living and active and sharper than any two-edged sword, and piercing as far as the division of soul and spirit, of both joints and marrow, and able to judge the thoughts and intentions of the heart."

The sword of the spirit is the Word of God, the scriptures. The sword is our offensive weapon. There is no power on earth stronger than the Word of God. It rightly divides the godly from the ungodly, the truth from the lies of the devil.

Spiritual warfare is part of the Christian's life, but despite the militant language our "war" has nothing to do with flesh and blood battles. We fight the enemy in prayer which is more powerful than physical weapons.

Our greatest battles are fought in our minds. Will you believe the enemy or the Lord? We fight in the name of Jesus and under the authority of the Almighty God of heaven and earth.

Deuteronomy20:1, **"When you go out to battle against your enemies and see horses and chariots *and* people more numerous than you, do not be afraid of them; for the LORD your God, who brought you up from the land of Egypt, is with you."**

- *Who or what are your enemies? Write them down. Thank the Lord for bringing you out of Egypt (your old way of life).*

_____

_____

_____

_____

_____

Isaiah 31:1, **"Woe to those who go down to Egypt for help, and rely on horses, who trust in chariots because they are many, and in horsemen because**

they are very strong, but who do not look to the Holy One of Israel, nor seek the Lord!"

Often we are tempted to look for answers in the world systems. Too often, we respond with ungodly tactics. Here are a few examples that may sound familiar:

1.) They hurt me deeply - I have a right to hurt them.

2.) They talk about me - I talk (gossip) about them.

3.) They cheated me - I'll get a lawyer and sue them.

4.) I'll gather all my friends together and we will gang up on them.

5.) They abused me, even did unspeakable things to me; I will never forgive.

6.) They insulted me; I had a right to be angry.
God get 'em.

All of us have experienced that heavy lump in our chest when we have been wronged or hurt. That has happened to me quite often, but when I surrender the situation to the Lord I am free of the ache inside. The problem may not have changed, but God gives me peace when I relinquish my will to His.

We may find it difficult to allow God to take over in our circumstances, but the alternative is bleak. The good news is God can handle things so much better than we can. He is our protection when we cannot defend ourselves.

God tells us many times in scripture that we are to trust in Him alone. Being Christians we should act accordingly. God's ways are not our ways, but when we trust in Him and do things His way (*not ours*), we will be blessed, experience peace and have power in our prayers.

Psalms 18:33-34, "He makes my feet like hinds' feet, and sets me upon my high places. He trains my hands for battle, so that my arms can bend a bow of bronze."

Recently, while on a trip to Colorado, we were amazed to see hinds climbing straight up the steep side of a rock cliff. Their cloven hoofs are designed to climb where their predators cannot go. God will equip you to rise above the mountains in your lives and to walk on the high places.

Do not be frightened or discouraged, for it is God who fights your battles. You can be assured God holds true to His promises. You must trust and pray and you will be able to overcome your most difficult of problems. Your part is to agree with Him in prayer, trust Him as you bend the bow of bronze, (as we pray, we send fiery arrows into the heart of our enemy).

2.) God fights for us.

<u>Psalms 144: 1-2,</u> **"Blessed be the Lord, my rock, Who trains my hands for war, and my fingers for battle; my lovingkindness and my fortress, my stronghold and my deliverer, my shield and He in whom I take refuge, Who subdues my people** (David's enemies) **under me."**

- *Pray this scripture back to the Lord and thank Him for His kindness and protection from the trials of life – from your enemies.*

<u>Psalms 144: 7-8,</u> **"Bow Your heavens, O Lord, and come down; touch the mountains, that they may smoke. Flash forth lightning and scatter them; send out Your arrows and confuse them. Stretch forth Your hand from on high; rescue me and deliver me out of great waters, out of the hand of aliens whose mouths speak deceit, and whose right hand is a right hand of falsehood."**

When I read this, I imagine myself standing on a mountain, looking down on a valley full of enemy armies. I raise my arms, waving them over the enemy and I can see the Lord coming down and destroying them.

Let us pray, Lord, "Rend the heavens and come down, annihilate the enemies of this nation." Bring light into the dark places, shine Your light on all the lies that people have believed about You." "God destroy the enemies of my family." You fill in the blank, "Lord, destroy_____ for Your glory, that men may see You and believe that You are the only Savior."

Psalms 20:6-7, "Now, I know that the Lord saves His anointed; He will answer him from His holy heaven with the saving strength of His right hand. Some trust in chariots, and some in horses; but we will remember the name of the Lord our God."

We don't have to rely on worldly weapons because the Holy Spirit will teach us how to fight our battles. He directs our prayers and He reveals to us the things that are on His heart, if we listen carefully. Our prayers become divinely powerful warfare when we agree with God for His will to be done. He will hear us from heaven and subdue our enemies.

Many times in my life, I have been totally helpless. I could not defend myself, heal myself, or change someone else's heart, but in the end, God was my defense, my healer, my deliverer. He was the miracle working God that saved me from my enemies.

C. Fight for our nation.

1.) Come let us reason together:

God has placed us in this nation for a reason. He desires is for us to pray and repent for the sins of this land. You may think, 'I haven't committed any of the horrible sins that I see all around me.' However, we are all part of America; we can identify with this nation and we all suffer because this country has become so ungodly. Many have become apathetic and so discouraged they no longer believe God will work on our behalf. This is a lie from the pit of hell that we need to recognize. We all need to believe what God has promised - He will fight for us if we will pray.

Isaiah 62:4-7, **"It will no longer be said to you, "Forsaken," Nor to your land will it any longer be said, "Desolate"; But you will be called, My delight is in her," And your land, "Married"; For the Lord delights in you, And to Him your land will be married. For as a young man marries a virgin, so your sons will marry you; And as the bridegroom rejoices over the bride, so your God will rejoice over you. On your walls, O Jerusalem, I have appointed watchmen; all day and all night they will never keep silent. You who remind the Lord, take no rest for yourselves; and give Him no rest until He establishes and makes Jerusalem a praise in the earth."**

Romans 11 tells us that we are grafted into the vine, Jesus. We are not natural Jews, but spiritual ones. Jesus came to save the Jews first and then the Gentiles. The scripture tells us we are adopted, grafted into His family.

Since America was dedicated to God from the beginning, we can pray this sample prayer from Isaiah for America as well as for Jerusalem:

- *V. 4, Thank You Lord that the peoples will no longer say, "There is no God in America." We will no longer be called desolate and abandoned by You, but we will be in covenant with You God. We shall be called the bride of the Most High God. Lord I know that our forefathers dedicated this nation to You; let no man, of government, take it from You.*

- *V.5 Lord, bring us to repentance so that we will stand holy and righteous before You, as a virgin stands before her husband. I pray that America will once again turn her heart to You and be pleasing to You.*

- *V.6, Let the praying men and women, prophets, watchmen and intercessors cry out night and day. Encourage them Lord so that they will pray without ceasing. May we never keep silent or take our rest until You, Lord, are glorified in the earth. I call out to You, be high and lifted up that all may see that You are God.*

D. Pray for Israel

1.) God loves Israel – so should we.

Genesis 12:2-3, "And I will make you a great nation, and I will bless you, and make your name great; and so you shall be a blessing; and I will bless those who bless you, and the one who curses you I will curse. And in you all the families of the earth will be blessed."

God is very clear that we should bless Israel. Praying for Israel is a great blessing to them and for us. They are a melting pot of cultures, religions and unbelievers similar to the U.S. Some are Jews in name only, they have no religion at all, but God has not given up on them. He will fulfill all of His promises to Israel. They are still His people, destined to glorify the Lord in all the earth. If we desire blessings, pray for the U.S. to remain a faithful ally to Israel.

Our President has moved our Embassy to Jerusalem officially recognizing it as the capital of Israel. He has gone against all of Israel's enemies who want to say Jerusalem does not belong to the Jews. I believe our nation will be blessed because of this decision by our President. God says that the Jews and Jerusalem belong to Him. When we agree with the Lord we will be blessed.

Isaiah 44: 1-3, "But now listen, O Jacob, My servant, and Israel, whom I have chosen: Thus says the Lord who made you and formed you from the womb, who will help you, 'Do not fear, O Jacob My servant; and you Jeshurun** (*a symbolic name for Israel, it is a token of affection, meaning* *dear, upright people*) **whom I have chosen. 'For I will pour out water on the thirsty land and streams on the dry ground; I will pour out My Spirit on your offspring, and My blessing on your descendants;'"**

Let's practice – Put the above scripture in your own words, write it out and pray it back to the Lord for Israel. (*Go ahead give it a try.*)

_____

_____

_____

_____

_____

_____

_____

_____

Isaiah 60:1-3, **"Arise, shine; for your light has come, and the glory of the Lord has risen upon**

you. "For behold, darkness will cover the earth and deep darkness the peoples; but the Lord will rise upon you and His glory will appear upon you. "Nations will come to your light, and kings to the brightness of your rising."

We can pray for Israel and America: "Arise Lord and shine Your light into all of the dark places in Israel (*America*). Let Your light shine with such glory that all peoples will see and be drawn to You. Lord there is great darkness covering the land, ungodliness and violence run rampant in the streets, but You are still God Almighty. Rise up, O God, and let Your kingdom come, Your will be done across the face of this land. Lord, establish Israel and call them by name in order to show the nations that there is one God in the earth. Let the nations see You and declare that You alone are God and that Israel belongs to You alone.

E. Hold out until the end.

Matthew 10:20, **"You will be hated by all because of My name, but it is the one who has endured to the end who will be saved."**

There are many places in scripture that the Lord admonishes us not to give up. The rewards from God are for those who hold out until the end. When we sin God commands us to repent, receive His forgiveness and continue trusting Him.

Matthew 24:11-14, "Many false prophets will arise
and will mislead many. Because lawlessness is
increased, most people's love will grow cold. But
the one who endures to the end, he will be saved.
This gospel of the kingdom shall be preached in
the whole world as a testimony to all the nations,
and then the end will come."

These are sobering words spoken by Jesus. Be careful
of those men and women who preach false doctrines
that feel good to our flesh, but are against the word of
God. Do not be misled, we should all take this
scripture seriously.

The world needs a Savior and because of God's great
love for us, he sent us Jesus. Not because of who we
are, but because of what Jesus has done, we now have
the authority in prayer to tear down the strongholds of
the enemy. He has given us the grace to preach the
good news to the lost and the power to endure.

I Timothy 1: 18, "This command I entrust to you,
Timothy, my son, in accordance with the
prophecies previously made concerning you, that
by them you fight the good fight."

God commands us to fight, whether we see ourselves
as warriors or not. What is the 'good fight'? Again I
say to you, fight smart – agree with God's word and
declare what He has to say about your situation. If you
don't know what the bible says, ask someone who
does know, a pastor or bible teacher.

Homework:

- **Day 1)** *Ask the Lord to show you the things that are on His heart. Take 10 minutes to listen. Write out what He impresses on you. (If you are not familiar with this type of prayer, don't be nervous. The Lord will start you off gently and the Holy Spirit will teach you step by step. If we love someone we should desire to make them happy.)*

_____

_____

_____

_____

_____

_____

_____

- *Day 2)* *Spend 10 minutes writing a prayer for Israel from Genesis 12:2-3*

_____

_____

_____

_____

_____

- *Day 3)* *Read and spend 10 minutes writing and praying for the United States from Psalm 71:1-6. As you pray change the emphasis from deliver me to deliver this nation.*

_____

_____

_____

_____

_____

- *Day 4)* Read Psalm 91 aloud – it will encourage you. Write out what the Lord says about you in this Psalm.

_____

_____

_____

_____

_____

- *Day 5)* Read Psalm 146 and spend 10 minutes praising the Lord. Write out your prayer.

_____

_____

_____

_____

_____

When the enemy whispers in your ear that you are not able to pray or make a difference, tell him what Jesus says about you. You are His beloved; He left all of heaven and came to earth to save you. Jesus says you are mighty in Him, that He loves you so much He lives in you and He holds you; you are seated in heavenly places with Him and you are held in the palm of His hand.

Be blessed dear ones, let the Lord encourage you. You are the apple of His eye; He delights in you.

How to Pray and Never Run Out of Words

Lesson 6

(All Scriptures are quoted from the New American Standard Version unless otherwise noted. All homework is in bold italics print.)

A. Declaring the Word of the Lord

1.) Agree with God's word and speak it aloud:

Romans 3:22-23, "But now apart from the Law the righteousness of God has been manifested, being witnessed by the Law and the Prophets, even the righteousness of God through faith in Jesus Christ for all those who believe; for there is no distinction; for all have sinned and fall short of the glory of God, …"

We are made righteous (in right standing with God) through Jesus Christ. It is not our merit that allows us to stand and pray before a Holy God. It is because of Jesus' sacrifice that we are made one with the Lord of the Universe. You can speak to the enemy and tell him that you are in right standing with God because of what Jesus did for you on the cross.

Ephesians 2: 4-6, "But God, being rich in mercy, because of His great love with which He loved us,

even when we were dead in our transgressions, made us alive together with Christ (by grace you have been saved), and raised us up with Him, and seated us with Him in the heavenly places in Christ Jesus, ..."

In **Lesson 2,** I talked about how Jesus fought the enemy by declaring what the Scriptures had to say about His situation. We must do the same. The enemy can't stand to hear God's word and when we declare the Scripture, we are using a powerful weapon against the enemy.

Declare that you are alive in Christ and seated with Him in heavenly places; you have favor and authority with God. Wow, what a realization – you are in Him. *(I know I want the Lord to live in me, but the idea that He wants me living in Him is beyond anything I can imagine. What a God!)*

Ephesians 2:7, **"For we are His workmanship, created in Christ Jesus for good works, which God prepared beforehand so that we would walk in them."**

When we fully grasp the great honor the Lord has bestowed upon us in Christ, we will live and pray differently. We each have the call of God on our lives. Your call is different from mine, but we are all called to pray. The Lord created us to be one with Him; furthermore, He prepared good works for us to walk in. Our Father needs each one of us to walk in those good works in order to fulfill His desires.

Matthew 16:19, "I will give you the keys of the kingdom of heaven; and whatever you bind on earth shall have been bound in heaven, and whatever you loose on earth shall have been loosed in heaven."

Satan does not want us to understand and live out this truth. Jesus' authority was not just for the apostles, but the church as well. God intends for us to use the authority He has given us. When we bind up sickness or any kind of evil, we are declaring God's will be done on earth. We can bind up the lies of the enemy and loose the truth of God's word. As we loose any of the purposes of God, they are released in heaven.

Matthew 12:29, "Or how can anyone enter the strong man's house and carry off his property, unless he first binds the strong man? And then he will plunder his house."

The strong man is symbolic for what is trying to hinder God's plans. It may be unbelief, hatred, alcoholism, drugs or any kind of perversion. We all need to learn to tell the enemy that he is bound in Jesus' name and he no longer has power over us, because the Living God resides in us. Tell the enemy that the Lord has free reign to work mightily in your situation.

Are you praying for someone who is lost? Bind up the strong man of unbelief. Bind up unbelief and wrong conceptions about God. Loose the truth of the Gospel to come into their hearts and minds. Bind up any anger or bitterness that is keeping them from the Lord and loose the love of God into their lives. Bind the lies that the enemy has told them and declare that they will hunger for truth in their innermost being. Tell the enemy that his days of controlling this person are over, the Lord Most High has paid the price for their soul and Jesus shall have what He paid for on the cross.

- *Now you try it - go on – say it out loud. Tell the enemy what the Lord has to say about your situation and declare God's will.*

2.) Praying for the church:

Colossians 3:13 – 16, (TLB) **"Be gentle and ready to forgive; never hold grudges. Remember, the Lord forgave you, so you must forgive others. Most of all, let love guide your life, for then the whole church will stay together in perfect harmony. Let the peace of heart that comes from Christ be always present in your hearts and lives, for this is your responsibility and privilege as members of his body. And always be thankful. Remember what Christ taught, and let his words enrich your lives and make you wise; teach them to each other and**

sing them out in psalms and hymns and spiritual songs, singing to the Lord with thankful hearts."

- *Mark this passage in your Bible and pray it often.*

We can pray this passage back to God concerning the church or any other believers. Paul talks about putting on the "new self". We are dead to sin and alive to Christ. Declare that the church shall be a powerful force working in harmony to bring about God's plans; that the world will see the love of Jesus in us and be drawn to Him. Proclaim that the church will arise and be a powerful force for change in our society, just as God intended us to be.

3.) God warns the church:

Revelation 3:15-19, "I know your deeds, that you are neither cold nor hot; I wish that you were cold or hot. So because you are lukewarm, and neither hot nor cold, I will spit you out of My mouth. Because you say, "I am rich, and have become wealthy, and have need of nothing," and you do not know that you are wretched and miserable and poor and blind and naked, I advise you to buy from Me gold refined by fire so that you may become rich, and white garments so that you may clothe yourself, and that the shame of your nakedness will not be revealed; and eye salve to anoint your eyes so that you may see. Those whom

I love, I reprove and discipline; therefore be zealous and repent."

In the Book of Revelation chapters 2-3 Jesus warns the churches that He is coming soon. He instructs them and us to hold fast until He comes. The letter to the Laodicean church is particularly scary. I don't think any of us would want to be spit out of God's mouth because we are lukewarm. The Lord warns us because He loves us and desires for us to fulfill His plans for the church.

Let us ask the Lord to forgive us for the greed and apathy that are prevalent in the church today. Bind up the spirits of hopelessness, apathy and greed.

The bible commentator, Matthew Henry says, "Part with sin and self-sufficiency, and come to Christ with a sense of your poverty and emptiness, that you may be filled with His hidden treasure."

- *Let's Pray: Lord, forgive us for being lukewarm and help us to recognize where we have been indifferent to You. I ask that the church would be on fire for You – that we will wake up and be the church You intended us to be. We are poor and wretched and recognize that only You have the Words of Life. Let us desire the heavenly riches and not be greedy for earthly things. We are poor and hopeless without You. Let the church desire to store up riches in heaven. May we be cleansed and clothed in Your garments of righteousness.*

- *I declare that the church of Jesus Christ shall live and give glory to the Most High God over all the earth. I declare that they shall stand and fight to tear down spiritual forces of darkness in high places; that they will shine the light of Jesus on all the dark places in the church. I declare that pastors, who are religious in name only, will be saved and delivered as well as those who sit in the pews, but are far from God. Let them declare Your gospel, Your good news of salvation to the lost and hurting.*

Do you get the idea? God wants us to pray; it's how He operates – through our free will. We can choose to obey and pray or we can miss what He desires for us.

4.) Pray for Israel:

God loves Israel and commands us to bless her so that we may be blessed. Now, you may ask yourself, 'Israel is so far removed from me, how can I make a difference to them?' We can support them by voting for the men and women who support Israel. We can support Christian ministries in Israel by prayer and with our finances. We can pray God's protection for them and pray that the Lord will reveal the Jewish Messiah to His people. We know the entire nation will not recognize Him until the end, but many individual

Jews are being saved everyday in Israel and in the U.S.

- *Let's do a little declaring: Lord Israel was created for Your glory. I declare today that they will not be destroyed by the enemies that surround them, but they will amaze the world with their strength and power that only comes from You. I declare that all Your promises to Israel will come to pass just as You say in Your Word. They shall possess all of the land that You gave to Abraham with an everlasting covenant that will not be broken. (Today they possess only a small portion of the land God originally gave them.)*

Jeremiah 29:11-14, "'For I know the plans that I have for you,' declares the Lord, 'plans for welfare and not for calamity to give you a future and a hope. Then you will call upon Me and come and pray to Me, and I will listen to you. You will seek Me and find Me when you search for Me with all your heart. I will be found by you,' declares the Lord, 'and I will restore your fortunes and will gather you from all the nations and from all the places where I have driven you,' declares the Lord, 'and I will bring you back to the place from where I sent you into exile.'"

In 1948, the Lord fulfilled this prophecy. The nation of Israel, was born in a day, by proclamation of the

U.N. God will keep every promise He ever made to Israel and to us.

Isaiah 66:8, "Who has heard such a thing? Who has seen such things? Can a land be born in one day? Can a nation be brought forth all at once?" As soon as Zion travailed, she also brought forth her sons."

Isaiah 41: 8-13, "But you, Israel, My servant, Jacob whom I have chosen, Descendant of Abraham My friend, You whom I have taken from the ends of the earth, and called from its remotest parts and said to you, 'You are My servant, I have chosen you and not rejected you.
'Do not fear, for I am with you; do not anxiously look about you, for I am your God. I will strengthen you, surely I will help you, surely I will uphold you with My righteous right hand.'
"Behold, all those who are angered at you will be shamed and dishonored; those who contend with you will be as nothing and will perish. "You will seek those who quarrel with you, but will not find them, those who war with you will be as nothing and non-existent. "For I am the Lord your God, who upholds your right hand, who says to you, 'Do not fear, I will help you.' "

- *We can pray: Thank You Lord, You have brought Your chosen people from around the world and given them a homeland of their own. Strengthen them and protect them from their enemies. I declare to Israel's enemies that they shall not shame Israel or destroy that land, because God is on their side, and it is He who upholds Israel. I read the end of the book – God wins.*

B. Always, begin and end with worship.

1.) Worship is the most powerful weapon we can use against the enemy:

The Psalms are filled with prayers of worship and praise to the Lord. Many of them begin by laying out the psalmist troubles to the Lord and end with I will trust in You Lord and worship You. The last five Psalms are nothing but worship. Pray them back to the Lord regularly, especially when you don't feel like praising the Lord. We need to train ourselves to live by faith and not out of our circumstances. I promise you will be content and at peace.

Psalm 119: 1-2, "How blessed are those whose way is blameless, who walk in the law of the Lord. How blessed are those who observe His testimonies, who seek Him with all their heart."

If you have never studied **Psalm 119,** I encourage you to do so. It is divided into sections, each one for a letter of the Hebrew alphabet. The psalmist is saying that the Lord is the Aleph and the Tav, the beginning and the end, (I*n Greek, we know it as the Alpha and*

Omega). He pours out his heart and asks the Lord to revive him while he dedicates himself to the Word of God.

Psalm 119:37-40, "Turn away my eyes from looking at vanity, and revive me in Your ways. Establish Your word to Your servant, as that which produces reverence for You. Turn away my reproach which I dread, for Your ordinances are good. Behold, I long for Your precepts; revive me through Your righteousness."

Psalm 119:105-107, "Your word is a lamp to my feet and a light to my path. I have sworn and I will confirm it, that I will keep Your righteous ordinances. I am exceedingly afflicted; revive me, O Lord, according to Your word."

When we are weary, we can turn to the Lord and He will revive us. God's word is our guide through life. Turn to Him and He will give you a heart of praise.

Psalm 69:30-32, "I will praise the name of God with song and magnify Him with thanksgiving. And it will please the Lord better than an ox or a young bull with horns and hoofs. The humble have seen it and are glad; you who seek God, let your heart revive."

Our sacrifices to God can be a good thing, but He would rather have our hearts. He desires us to be humble before Him and obey.

Remember **2 Chronicles 20:20b-22, Jehoshaphat stood and said, "Listen to me, O Judah and inhabitants of Jerusalem, put your trust in the Lord your God and you will be established. Put your trust in His prophets and succeed." When he had consulted with the people, he appointed those who sang to the Lord and those who praised Him in holy attire, as they went out before the army and said, "Give thanks to the Lord, for His lovingkindness is everlasting." When they began singing and praising, the Lord set ambushes against the sons of Ammon, Moab and Mount Seir, who had come against Judah; so they were routed. For the sons of Ammon and Moab rose up against the inhabitants of Mount Seir destroying them completely; and when they had finished with the inhabitants of Seir, they helped to destroy one another.**

Wow, isn't that what we want - to win a battle without wielding a sword and it took them three whole days to carry off the spoils. Our spoils are seeing our loved ones saved and seeing God glorified in this nation, Israel and the nations of the earth. Our greatest reward is to see the Lord high and lifted up in all of His glory.

2.) To obey is better than sacrifice:

I Samuel 15:22, "Samuel said, 'Has the Lord as much delight in burnt offerings and sacrifices, as in obeying the voice of the Lord? Behold, to obey is better than sacrifice and to heed than the fat of rams.'"

Our obedience and worship are pleasing to the Lord. Keep in mind, the enemy cannot stand to hear you praise the Lord. Obedience to the Lord will defeat your adversary every time.

3.) The Lord will give you strength for each new day:

Isaiah 40: 28-31, "Do you not know? Have you not heard? The everlasting God, the Lord, the Creator of the ends of the earth does not become weary or tired. His understanding is inscrutable. He gives strength to the weary, and to him who lacks might He increases power. Though youths grow weary and tired, and vigorous young men stumble badly, yet those who wait for the Lord will gain new strength; they will mount up with wings like eagles, they will run and not get tired, they will walk and not become weary."

When we are weary, we can trust in the Lord to fight for us. Our God is Holy, Almighty, All Powerful, Lord of the Heavens and the Earth. He is worthy to be obeyed and to be worshipped.

C. My prayer for you

I pray you will use what you have discovered in this study everyday and that you will learn to <u>fight smart</u>. You are not a victim to be tossed about by the enemy, but you are a child of the Most High God. You have power and authority, in Jesus, over Satan who was defeated by the death and resurrection of Christ the King.

Jesus paid it all, a price that we could never pay, so that we can be set free from sin and eternal death. Receive His marvelous gift and be liberated to live life abundantly.

May the Lord guide you and direct your path; may He bless your coming in and your going out. May you find favor with God and be pleasing to Him. May He be glorified through you.

<u>Numbers 6:24-26,</u> "'The Lord bless you, and keep you; the Lord make His face shine on you, and be gracious to you; the Lord lift up His countenance on you, and give you peace.'"

List of Topical Scriptures to Pray

Praise

Psalms:
8: 1-9
18:1-19
84
103:1-22
145:1-21
146:1-10
147:1-20
148
149
150

Trust in God

Psalms:
27:1-14
3: 1-8
4:1-8
Habakkuk:
3:17-19

Mercy in times of trouble

Psalms:
6:1-10
7:1-17
13:1-6
17:1-15
26:1-12
37:1-40
102

WhenI am Worried

Psalms:
27:1-14
31:14-24
40:1-8
86:1-17
Philippians:
4:4-9

Prayer for the lost

Acts:
15:7-11
2: 38-40
9:7-10
Romans:
5:15-18
6:16-23
8:31-39
10:13-17

Prayer for believers

Ephesians:
1:16-19
5:6-17
Colossians:
1:9-12
3:12-17
1 Thess.:
3:11-13

List of Topical
Scriptures to Pray

Pray for church
Psalms:
43:1-5
Colossians:
3:13-16
Revelation:
3:15-19

Pray for America
Psalms:
10:1-18
20:1-9
21:7-13
33:12-22
85:1-13
Isaiah:
60:1-3
I Chronicles:
16:22-36
17:20-27

Pray for Israel
Psalms:
22:19-24
99:1-9
129:1-8
Isaiah:
41:8-13
62:1-3
41:8-16
Jeremiah:
29:11-14

Made in the USA
Columbia, SC
15 November 2023

26383510R00061